WHERE CROSS THE CROWDED WAYS

WHERE CROSS THE CROWDED WAYS

Prayers of a City Pastor

ERNEST T. CAMPBELL

Author of *Christian Manifesto*

ASSOCIATION PRESS

NEW YORK

WHERE CROSS THE CROWDED WAYS

International Standard Book Number: 0–8096–1861–3
Library of Congress Catalog Card Number: 73–9792

Library of Congress Cataloging in Publication Data

Campbell, Ernest T.
    Where cross the crowded ways.

    1. Prayers. I. Title.
BV245.C26   242'.8   73–9792
ISBN 0–8096–1861–3

This book is dedicated to the work and vision of Caesar Chavez, and all royalties have been assigned to the United Farm Workers' National Union.

A City-Dweller's Prayer

O God of every time and place,
  prevail among us too;
Within the city that we love
  its promise to renew.
Our people move with downcast
  eyes, tight, sullen and afraid;
Surprise us with Thy joy divine,
  for we would be remade.

O Thou whose will we can resist,
  but cannot overcome,
Forgive our harsh and strident ways,
  the harm that we have done.
Like Babel's builders long ago
  we raise our lofty towers,
And like them, too, our words
  divide, and pride lays waste our
  powers.

Behind the masks that we maintain
  to shut our sadness in,
There lurks the hope, however dim,
  to live once more as men.
Let wrong embolden us to fight,
  and need excite our care;
If not us, who? If not now, when?
  If not here, God, then where?

Our fathers stayed their minds on
  Thee in village, farm and plain;
Help us, their crowded, harried kin,
  no less Thy peace to claim.
Give us to know that Thou dost love
  each soul that Thou hast made;
That size does not diminish grace,
  nor concrete hide Thy gaze.

Grant us, O God, who labor here
  within this throbbing maze,
A forward-looking, saving hope
  to galvanize our days.
Let Christ, who loved Jerusalem,
  and wept its sins to mourn,
Make just our laws and pure our
  hearts; so shall we be reborn!
                    Amen.

About These Prayers

One does not easily release his Sunday prayers to the printed page. Only the urgings of friends and colleagues in several congregations could induce the required nerve.

I have deliberately cast these prayers in Elizabethan English. Not that the King James language is the only tongue God hears, but because I have deep misgivings about those liberties with prayer so fashionable today in which transcendence is compromised by means of grammatical and verbal intimacy with the Divine. I deem it more important that God be our Lord than our pal.

A word probably needs to be said about the original setting of these prayers. At The Riverside Church, we subdivide the traditional pastoral prayer into three sections: Thanksgiving, Intercession and Petition. Each section closes with the phrase "Through Jesus Christ our Lord" after which the congregation is encouraged to respond with an audible "Amen." It is important that our prayers for others (intercession) precede our prayers for ourselves (petition). One cannot pray for the starving homeless of some flood-ravaged island in the South Seas and calmly move on to ask God to help him get a new car. Intercession performs a monitoring service for petition. It is an essential link between Thanksgiving and Petition.

It should also be said that these prayers reflect the conviction that the pastoral prayer each week can be deeply meaningful if the leader takes it seriously and works at it. When a man wishes to invigorate his parish, his mind commonly turns to ways of scheduling the unusual: the weekend retreat, the visiting preacher, some musical extravaganza, a widely heralded dramatic production, a service in which strobe lights, modern sounds and updated litanies are featured, the dialog sermon.

It is wiser, I believe, to *energize the usual* than to *schedule the unusual*—that is, to look more to doing better those functions of the ministry that are basic to our calling: leading worship, preaching the word, visiting, counseling, administering the business and program of the church. To slight these fundamental services while casting about for some gala event that will provide instant invigoration is to forget that the ordinary over the years has proved more useful to God than the spectacular. One of these "ordinary" responsibilities, I am convinced, is the preparation of what is usually referred to as the pastoral prayer.

There was a time in my ministry when I did not view the matter so. Early upon graduation from seminary, however, I took frequent opportunity to worship under the leadership of George Buttrick at the Madison Avenue Presbyterian Church in New York City. I confess that his pastoral prayers had a way of making my eyes glisten with tears of joy and penitence. From such experiences I came to see that I had underestimated the importance of public prayer. An eagerness to preach had led me to short-change my preparation for the Sunday prayers. To this day, I spend more time on these prayers proportionately than I do on the weekly sermon. My experience as a pastor convinces me of the soundness of this emphasis.

In addition, I should like to testify that for myself I have found their preparation a rewarding devotional experience each week. During the hours of preparation, I find myself strangely open to God and singularly aware of the range and depth of my people's needs. It is this which makes me dare to hope that they will translate easily into prayers for personal devotion.

As this book goes to press, one has the distinct impression that a new hunger for the transcendent is abroad in the land. The vertical dimension of life is again asserting its claims. Even the most flamboyant secularism cannot fully stifle the human need to pray. This discovery may yet be the most significant fact of the 1970's.

ERNEST T. CAMPBELL

AS A HEN GATHERS HER BROOD

Our fathers stayed their minds on Thee
in village, farm and plain;
Help us, their crowded, harried kin,
no less Thy peace to claim.

I

O Thou who didst make us to pass our years in freedom, show
Thyself merciful to us, for we are tightly wound, boxed in, prisoners
of our illusions, and, in the main, a nervous, dreary and joyless lot.

The goals we seek have robbed us of our wonder, and the machines
we worship reduced us to a crowd of look-alike consumers.
> Here on this Thy day, through the vehicle of praise, grant that
> what is dead in us may come alive.

We thank Thee for family roots and ties:
> for the look of trust in the faces of our children;
> for songs that penetrate the darkest night;
> for hope that will not be absorbed even by our doubt.

Drive us, by a gnawing hunger for the real, outside the inn, until
within the homely timbers of the stable we sight the Christ and find
our souls made tall and free again in contemplation of Thy love.

Through Jesus Christ our Lord.

II

Hear us now, O Lord, as we pray for New York City; pray for it,
not from without, as though its dust and noise and pain were beneath us or beyond, but from within, as those who know its squeeze
and take to heart its burned-out hopes and facelessness.

Grant that fences that keep potential friends apart may be fash-
ioned into bridges so that the hurts of any may be the concern of all.

Help us to look for Thee and find Thee in the life we live and the
work we do.

> If we take the IRT and ride to the edges of Van Cortlandt Park,
> Thou art there.
> If we shuttle our way into the milling density of Times Square,
> Thou art there.

If we ride to the uppermost reaches of the Empire State Building, even there shall Thy hand lead us and Thy right hand hold us.

If in the dead of night we feel deserted and depressed, the darkness hideth not from Thee; for the light shineth as the day.

O God, for whom all times and places are Thy habitation, be Thou our God for we would be Thy people.

Through Jesus Christ our Lord.

III

As we look to the world within we are prompted to lay our many needs before Thee. In the light of our Saviour's birth we ask for power to overcome whatever in us runs counter to His love, and for courage to be loyal to the light He came to share.

May His lowliness curb our status-seeking,
His humility melt away our pride,
His purity condemn our lust,
His love for people shame the love we waste on things,
His sense of mission challenge our aimlessness.

Give us feeling for those whose lot in life is harder than our own, and a particular concern for those who live and die as though Christ has not come, who do not know that at the heart of things love reigns, and heaven cares.

All which we pray,
through Jesus Christ our Lord. *Amen.*

I

Eternal God, our Father, help us in these precious moments of common prayer to forget the style of our dress, our plans for the day, and any momentary affliction that would make us more conscious of self than Thee, to the end that we may pray with singleness of mind and from the heart.

We thank Thee for all that keeps us believing that our years have meaning:
>   that a knowing, caring hand is at the helm;
>   that the resounding fury of the nations is not the final sound;
>   that love endures when tongues have ceased and prophecies have
>   failed.

We thank thee for ages past and ages still to come,
>   for the wisdom of Scripture,
>   the means of grace,
>   the bonds of faith,
>   and hope that springs from the eternal and fills our hearts.

Let a sense of Thy goodness course through every fiber of our being until our lips declare Thy praise.

Through Jesus Christ our Lord.

I I

We pray, Lord, for our city, Thy gift to us:
>   rich in buildings but, oh, so poor in soul;
>   high in crime and low in morale;
>   a playground for some and a nightmare for many;
>   gateway to the nation, but road's end for those too drugged, too
>   poor, too tired to get up and try again.

We pray for our mayor, our chief of police, our civil magistrates, our planners and advisors,

that in these crisis years they may govern and direct us with
wisdom, boldness and imagination.

Let the stark prospect of a shared demise unite all who would build
against those who would destroy.

And, if it please Thee, God, let Thy saving grace so reach and
ransom every heart,
    that our homes may be joyful,
    our streets safe,
    our laws just,
    our pleasures pure,
    and our will to make things right indomitable.

Through Jesus Christ our Lord.

III

We pray, lastly, for ourselves, bearing as individuals and as a
church the marks of a culture that is too much with us.
    So tune our responses to human need that we may reflect Thy
      spirit rather than the spirit of the age.
    So deliver us from cant and hypocrisy that our yea may be yea
      and our nay nay.
    So free us from the need to justify ourselves that others may be
      at ease in our presence, and our own hearts at peace.

Bless this congregation with Thy loving-kindness, that here on
this hill that cannot be hid we may continue to raise a consistent,
costly and contagious witness to the truth that sets men free.

All which we pray in faith and with thanksgiving,
    through Jesus Christ our Lord. *Amen.*

I

Because we did not make ourselves;
Because we do not keep ourselves;
Because we cannot forgive ourselves;
    Our hearts reach out to Thee, O God.
We thank Thee for our creation, preservation and redemption:
    for hills to climb,
    burdens to carry,
    temptations to resist,
    and fears to overcome.
We thank Thee for all that helps us in our pilgrimage:
    the remembrance of those who walked this way before us and
        did it well;
    signs of Thy presence, often in unlikely places, giving us to know
        that we are not alone;
    the unanswerable logic of lives given over to Thy service in
        selfless love;
    the work of Thy Holy Spirit in our minds and hearts, uniting
        for us the Jesus of history and the Christ of faith.
With all that lies within us we would acclaim Thy goodness and
speak Thy praise,
    through Jesus Christ our Lord.

I I

We pray today for all those who seek as Christians to make this
towering metropolis mindful of Thy presence:
    concerned believers, at work in radio and television, to rescue
        the public airways from their bondage to puerility and greed;
    those in the judicial process who believe that justice partakes of
        the eternal, and labor in that light;
    businessmen who shun the shoddy product and the inflated price
        in an effort to serve the public well;
    librarians and museum keepers who delight in making their
        wares available for the flowering of our humanity;
    policemen who enforce the law fairly and with understanding;

those in the performing arts who waken in us the good and
  beautiful and true;
prison chaplains who quietly make their rounds each day, com-
  municating hope;
parents in our crowded slums who defy their grim surroundings
  and secure their children in a love that will not quit.

Help these, and others like them, to keep at it. And through their
several ministries, gracious Father, may a city find its soul again,
  through Jesus Christ our Lord.

III

Play the light of Thy truth upon our less-than-perfect hearts, O
Lord; for, left to our own understanding, we have a way of be-
friending sin and opposing righteousness.

Help those who pass through heavy seas to ride out the storm.

By Thy providence lead those who are down on themselves into
some life experience in which their worth will be affirmed.

Call back to Thy side those who can recall a day when they loved
Thee more.

And for those who weep the tears of the bereaved, renew the vision
of earth's first Easter that they may conceive of death henceforth
as one of the "all things" that work together for our good.

Keep us faithful to each other and to Thee, whatever comes, until
on Thy strong arms we fall, and our work is done.

Through Jesus Christ our Lord. *Amen.*

I

Eternal God, our Father, beneath whose rule we live and in whose grace we stand, with all that is within us we would bless Thy holy name. We thank Thee for the constants in our life:

> that the ground is firm beneath our tread;
> that day follows night;
> that the seasons march in predictable succession;
> that the gates of mercy are ever open to us in our need.

We thank Thee for all that is new and changing in our life:

> for startling breakthroughs in the realm of science;
> for the audibility of people too long silent, and the visibility of wrongs too long concealed;
> for experimentation in the arts, and in particular the art of public worship;
> for new people next door or up the street, and the prospect of contributing to each other's growth.

O Thou whose ways are from of old and yet whose works are ever new, make us grateful for the past and open toward the future.

Through Jesus Christ our Lord.

I I

We join our prayers to hold before Thee this city of bright lights and broken hearts—a comedy to those who think; but to those who feel, a tragedy.

Grant to our mayor and those who share his rule the patience needed to contend with the clamor of competing voices, and the ability to hear this clamor as the language of democracy.

Raise up in us, the people, the willingness to break with private goals often enough and long enough to ease some burden or to right some wrong.

Give us a new confidence in due process as a means of getting where we want to go, and the good sense to use our power, personal and conferred, with modesty and restraint.

Through Jesus Christ our Lord.

III

We pray now for ourselves, acknowledging that
    our lost radiance,
    our much fretting,
    our tell-tale tensions,
discredit the faith we profess and dishonor Thee. Renovate us,
O Lord, through the tireless workings of Thy Holy Spirit,
    until all in us that is unworthy of the King may fall away,
    and Christ rule unrivaled in our hearts.

Work Thy will through us, O Lord.
If not; Thy will be done through others.

All which we pray through Jesus Christ our Lord. *Amen.*

I

We find Thy name upon our lips, O God, for Thou hast placed it in our hearts. However much we twist and turn and run to flee from Thy great love, we sense in the inmost citadel of our being that we have no future save the future that we know in Thee.

For minds that can think;
For hearts that can feel;
For hands and feet that can do;
    We thank Thee.

For large purposes that call us;
For associations and causes that unite us;
For grace that restores and forgives;
    We thank Thee.

In a day when the problems that confront us seem more than we can handle, open our eyes to the resources at our command as children of the king, and make us grateful.

Through Jesus Christ our Lord.

II

We pray for all who find this city a place of bitterness and a wilderness of fear:
    those who came with hopes that have long since been abandoned;
    those who came with high ideals and long now to recover them;
    those who came with outstretched arms who now leave unexpressed their need for other people.

Nor would we forget:
    those who are trapped in jobs that slowly eat away their life;
    those who want to change the city, but don't know how;
    those for whom the dawn of each new day calls them to resume a war of nerves against a system that keeps them on the outside looking in.

O Thou who art able to demolish the old and bring the new to birth, work Thou in this our town and make us agents of our brother's good and the glory of Thy name.

Through Jesus Christ our Lord.

III

Our names and needs are known to Thee, O Lord. Behind our Sunday clothes and manners lie unruly kingdoms of fierce ambition, shameful pride, and passions that we hope will never see the light of day.

Where we shout the loudest we are most insecure,
Where we have betrayed Thee most grievously we are most defensive.
Where we have sensed and done Thy will most fully we are largely unaware,
and our witness is the stronger for it.

Help us to see each other as people. Let the love of Christ so rule our hearts that each may think of the other first, and all of us live to adorn the gospel of the crucified and risen Christ.

These prayers we offer unto Thee through the same Jesus Christ our Lord. *Amen.*

I

O Thou who art our maker and our God, the giver and sustainer of life, we would bless Thy name at all times. Thy praise would continually rise from our grateful hearts.

We thank Thee that Thy power extends beyond man's prowess and achievements,
> that our towers never do quite touch the sky,
> that always Thou art more than we have thought or preached Thee to be.

We thank Thee that a fall of snow can hobble a mighty city,
> that strong headwinds can slow our jets and make us late,
> that heavy rains can force a cancellation of public events,
> that high seas command the respect of our sturdiest ocean-going ships.

In short, we thank Thee, God, for everything and anything that humbles us before the mystery of life and keeps us from the folly of worshipping the works of our own hands. Thou alone art God and together we would bless Thy holy name.

Through Jesus Christ our Lord.

I I

Be pleased to hear us, Lord, as we pray for this city and its inhabitants:

Teach us how to add community to proximity;
> how better to use all the time we save by not having to commute;
> how to ward off hostility by running the risk of letting our humanity come through;
> how to relate the sermon on the mount to life on the hill or in the valley.

Give us the good sense to ignore the oratory of the hatemonger, and keep us so honest about our own sin as to rise above the need for scapegoats.

Bless those in authority over us with patience and understanding, with loyal colleagues and citizens who care.

And guide the inhabitants of this renowned metropolis into paths of meaningful service and courageous action.

Through Jesus Christ our Lord.

III

O Thou whose will for us is life and not death:
  forgive us the blindness and perversity that keep us from choosing life;
  help us to act on the truth we know lest we lose it and fall back;
  spare us the hypocrisy of assuming that our convictions are objectively pure while our brother's point of view is slanted with self-interest;
  when our grasp of Thee is weak, keep firm Thy hold on us;
  when what Thou art is most hidden from our eyes, help us to cling to what Thou dost command.
  May it be our joy and uppermost intention
    to rest in Thee,
    to work for Thee,
    to become like Thee.

Through Jesus Christ our Lord.   *Amen.*

I

Proud men that we are, O God, we tend to blame our failures on others and take sole credit for our achievements. Show us how wrong we are on both counts, and move our stubborn souls to praise Thee as they ought.

We thank Thee for cooling breezes on a warm day,
    for the ability to taste and digest food,
    for the renewing quality of sleep,
    and the rhythm of work and rest.
We thank Thee for time in its flow,
    the seasons in their march,
    the stars in their courses.
But most we thank Thee for Thy life within us, binding us to one another and to Thee:
    for signs in the most unlikely places that Thou art on the premises;
    for unforgettable moments when Thy glory possessed us fully and paled all else before it;
    for occasions without number when word or sacrament or both kept our feet from falling and our faith from giving out.

O Thou who art more to us than all Thy gifts combined, Thy name be here and everywhere adored by us and by all men.

Through Jesus Christ our Lord.

II

We pray today for those in our society who have direct personal contact with men and women, and boys and girls, weighted down with problems:
    the social worker, trying to build solvency and hope into families that cannot make it on their own;
    the policeman, called at the eleventh hour to a scene of strife and danger to settle a dispute he did not cause;

the judge in his chambers quietly interpreting to children the
meaning of a divorce just granted;

the librarian attempting to awaken an interest in serious reading
in young minds addicted to TV;

the guidance counselor pleading with a would-be dropout to
give it another try;

the doctor nurturing the will to live for patients in the sunset
years;

the church-school teacher using every skill of mind and imagination to bring her students to faith in Jesus Christ.

Encourage them in their work, O Lord, lest in a world of complex
systems and distorted values they should feel their work in vain.

Through Jesus Christ our Lord.

III

O Thou who art busy with every man, believing in us more fully
than we dare to believe in ourselves, grant us what we need to be
more like Jesus:

a quiet mind,

a forgiving spirit,

indifference to wealth,

a humbler estimate of self,

a readiness to pray,

a clearer vision of Thy purposes,

courage to do the right we know.

Command us and comfort us, O God, for we need both direction
and consolation. Then shall our ordered lives confess the beauty
of Thy peace.

Through Jesus Christ our Lord. *Amen.*

I

O Thou who art at once the joy of heaven and the hope of earth, whose goodness never fails, bless us with a due sense of Thine unstinting grace, that we may enthusiastically hail and magnify Thy name.

We thank Thee for our ties to generations past and generations still to come,
    for our ability to identify with one another,
    for our vulnerability to truth and our capacity for reason.

We thank Thee for good health and length of days,
    for friends who seem always to appear when courage wanes,
    for unarguable seasons of prayerful intimacy with Thee,
    for a Christ who both comforts and confronts.

Dissolve for us the semblance of any notion that we are a self-made people. Teach us the measure of our indebtedness, that we may praise Thee more nearly as we ought.

Through Jesus Christ our Lord.

II

We pray today for New York City:
    a microcosm of the ailments and aspirations of the world;
    a representative sampling of western man at his best and worst;
    an ordeal for many, a delight for some.

Raise us as a people, Gracious Father, into a community in which the welfare of one becomes the concern of all. Give us to see our differences as assets rather than liabilities, occasions for growth rather than grounds for tension. Out of our teeming multitudes grant that a new breed of man may surface for whom the common good will inspire nobler forms of public service.

Bless the police commissioner of our city with decision-making wisdom, and an irrevocable commitment to the equitable enforcement of law. Help us as members of Christ's body to more effectively relate our faith to life as it is lived around us. Make us bearers of hope, champions of justice, and agents of reconciliation.

Through Jesus Christ our Lord.

III

We are both terrified and comforted in the knowledge that while men look on the outward appearance, Thou dost look on the heart:
> terrified that our masks and poses are transparent to Thee; that our human gamesmanship is lost on Thee; that our inmost desires are billboard clear to Thine all-seeing sight.
> yet comforted as well in the assurance that Thou dost understand the good intention that fails to materialize in action; the sentiments of gratitude that never come to speech; the essential humbleness of spirit that so often masquerades behind a false bravado.

O Thou whose love is less a love "because" and more a love "in spite of," let the remembrance of Thy grace make us more authentically human and more dependably serviceable to Thee, for we pray in faith, and with thanksgiving.

Through Jesus Christ our Lord. *Amen.*

I

It is good for us to bless Thy name, O God; to remember Thy mercies every morning and Thy loving-kindness every night. The world is so much with us that we gauge our wealth by the wrong things: property owned, money amassed, securities held, people impressed. And thus come short of knowing how rich we really are.

We praise Thee for life's intangibles:
    the lift of a loving voice,
    the warmth of a child's confidence,
    the strength that comes from an accepted sorrow,
    the excitement of a shared purpose.

We praise Thee most for faith that lights our way:
    for everything in us that urges us to call Thee Father;
    for all that hints Thy presence in our fevered world;
    and for the gift unspeakable, Thine only Son, full of grace and
        truth.

Move us to speak the thanks we feel, and forgive our much complaining.

Through Jesus Christ our Lord.

II

Hear us now, O Lord, as we pray for our neighboring institutions in the Morningside community: St. Luke's Hospital, Barnard, Teachers College, Columbia, the Manhattan School of Music, Woodstock, Union and Jewish Theological Seminaries, P.S. 125, Corpus Christi School and Church, the International House, the Interchurch Center, and sister congregations of various traditions:
    Bless them in their several roles and services and grant that
        the sheer routine of their day-by-day existence may blind
        neither them nor us to the vision that gave them birth.

Make us grateful for each other's presence, open to each other's
needs, careful of each other's rights, and happy for each
other's gains.

Through Jesus Christ our Lord.

III

And now, as a people of many cares and needs, we pray for ourselves.

We have engineered our friendships and manipulated those we
love.

We have shouted loudest when most insecure, and pinned the
blame for what we are on every door but our own.

Cleanse us, O God, and help us to presevere in every good intention in the knowledge that all things are possible to him who be-
lieves.

Bless our life together in this church. Help us to clarify our convictions, to subordinate personal whims and private fears to the
larger goals of Christ.

As Thou hast dealt with us in overflowing grace, so may we give
ourselves to Thee with generous abandon, and make available to
our Father's Kingdom the best and most we have of time and sub-
stance and ability.

Through Jesus Christ our Lord.   *Amen.*

ALL SORTS AND CONDITIONS OF MEN

Behind the masks that we maintain
to shut our sadness in,
There lurks the hope, however dim,
to live once more as men.

I

Let it not be, O God, that praise should rise to Thee from all places of Thy dominion while we hold our peace. Charge our being with the currents of gratitude, that whatever be our momentary mood or fortune, we may find cause to bless Thy name.

We thank Thee for patience that helps us bridge desire and fulfillment;
> for unwise prayers that went unanswered, sparing us heavy pain;
> for the unwelcome new that led us to discover in ourselves capacities we never dreamed were there;
> for ancient words of Scripture that blaze with light and meaning as our circumstances change;
> for the winsomeness of Jesus that excites the trust of young and old in every generation;
> and for Thy mercy that holds us fast even when we are hardly worth the holding.

Let the joy of what Thou art indwell our souls, that even in the worst of times our hearts may sing Thy praise.

Through Jesus Christ our Lord.

I I

We pray today for those among us, and in the world around us, who are burdened not by too little but by too much:
> those who have so much power that they have grown indifferent to the rights and claims of others, and are fast becoming what they do not wish to be;
> those who have so much health that they cannot understand the sick or reckon adequately with their own mortality;
> those who have so much wealth that they prize possessions more than people, and worry into the night about losing what they have;

those who have so much knowledge that they have grown proud
and self-sufficient and lost the common touch;
those who have so much virtue that they cannot see their sins
or appreciate Thy grace;
those who have so much leisure that they move like driftwood
on the surface of existence, lacking any cause larger than
themselves.

O Thou who art able to save us from abundance or privation, meet
the strong in their strength. Possess them in the fullness of their
powers, that what they have and what they are may be conscripted
for Thy service, wherein is peace.

Through Jesus Christ our Lord.

III

With yearnings that we cannot fully identify, much less describe;
with fears too personal to voice; harboring hostilities of which we
are ashamed; and weighted with a sense of guilt for having done
so little with so much; we make bold now to pray for ourselves:
teach us what it means to live in Thee,
to rest in Thee,
to hope in Thee;
let Thy presence fill those homes where death has come;
let Thy wisdom fall like a gentle rain on the parched souls of
all who are confused;
let Thy warming, healing light kindle trust in those who are sick
or in any way afflicted;
let Thy joy overcome the dolefulness of those who have forgot-
ten how to laugh.

Shape Thy grace around our inmost needs, O God. Give us not
over to ourselves. Strive with us yet a little longer, for we love Thee
and would serve Thee fully.

Through Jesus Christ our Lord. *Amen.*

I

We thank Thee, God, that praise is therapy, and gratitude the medicine of the soul. At least for the time it takes to pray, we would set our minds on Thy mercies and give up feeling sorry for ourselves. Thou hast blest us with the gift of life:
  surrounded us with friends;
  trusted us with responsibility;
  endowed us with conscience;
  provided us with all things needful;
  and set Thy love upon us.

Here within the quiet of this hour, we would remember those whose sacrifices have secured the good that we enjoy:
  parents, teachers, soldiers;
  artists, inventors, crusaders;
  scholars, pioneers and prophets.
Chiefly we would remember Jesus Christ:
  His selfless life;
  His voluntary death;
  His victorious resurrection;
  and His continuing power to save.

Our praises rise to Thee, from whence our blessings come.

Through Jesus Christ our Lord.

II

We embrace in our prayers today those who live with a sense of running out of what they need:
  those who are running out of time, their dreams still unfulfilled;
  those who are running out of patience, wondering how long they can endure;
  those who are running out of health, who feel their powers waning day by day;

those who are running out of money, fighting growing costs on
    fixed incomes;
those who are running out of excuses, and nearing the time when
    they must assume the blame for their failures;
those who are running out of faith, having borrowed too much
    and too long from others;
those who are running out of love, finding it easier all the time
    to accuse and criticize and hate.
O Thou who alone art able to keep us from falling, whose power
is unbounded; where our reserves are low, fill us again, for we
would endure all the way to the very end.

Through Jesus Christ our Lord.

III

We pray now for this church:
    its officers and members,
    its ministers,
    its varied publics,
    its impact on the city roundabout.
Give us, we pray, a lively sense of mission:
    the ability to choose priorities;
    the grace to deal creatively with differences;
    the hope that belongs to the gospel;
    the faith to believe, when to doubt or disbelieve would be the
        easier way.
Let it be enough for us that we have seen the Christ and heard
His call; lest, craving the good opinion of the world or our own
comfort, we should leave undone the work entrusted to our care.

We seek, now let us find;
We ask, let it now be given unto us;
We knock, open Thou, O God, the door.

Through Jesus Christ our Lord. *Amen.*

I

O Thou who art above us, around us and within; to whom we belong as to no other; from whom we turn only when we are deceived; beneath the lazing sun of summer, as in the chill of winter, we would praise Thy Holy Name:

We thank Thee for the constancy of loyal friends,
    the company of good books,
    the pleasing sounds of music,
    and ripples of laughter that limit our pretensions.
We thank Thee for the goodly heritage we enjoy as Christians:
    hymns that speak our thoughts of Thee;
    the bread broken and the cup shared;
    a sense of continuity with those who followed in another day;
    our connections with brave warriors in the present who fight the
        age-old fight of faith on a thousand different fronts.
We thank Thee most for Jesus the Christ:
    the life he lived,
    the death he died,
    his presence with us now.

Blessing and honor, dominion and power be unto Thee, our God.

Through Jesus Christ our Lord.

I I

We pray today for those in our society who near the breaking point:
    those who are expected to produce more than they can deliver;
    those whose inner grief and loneliness have plunged the heart
        in darkness;
    those who need work but find the market tight;
    those whose every breath is drawn in a struggle against some
        dread disease;

those who have been repeatedly rebuffed because of color;
those who await the release of imprisoned loved ones;
those who slowly inched from Thee and suffer now the pain of
   a remembered gladness.
O Thou who art able to keep that which we have committed unto
Thee, impart to the sorely pressed the courage to hang on yet one
day more. Let Thy strength be ministered to them according to
their need and Thy boundless grace.

Through Jesus Christ our Lord.

III

As part of our worship and our reasonable service, we pray now for
one another. Who of us is free of pride?
   of fear?
   of broken promises?
   of wavering enthusiasm?
   of pettiness and petulance?
   of disloyalty to Christ?

Pardon us, O God, singly and together:
   If we be sunshine soldiers, weatherize our souls that we may
      serve Thee well in any season.
   If we be overly enamored of our works, impress on us the
      primacy of grace.
   If we have lost Thee in a changing world that won't stand still,
      help us to know Thee again as the same from age to age, a
      faithful presence, the God who keeps covenant.

Ask, O God, and it shall be given Thee;
Knock, and it shall be opened unto Thee;
for Thou art indeed our light and our salvation,
and we have no life save the life we know in Thee.

Through Jesus Christ our Lord. *Amen.*

I

Lord, look upon Thy people as they pray, with mercy and fore-bearance; for we are a puzzle to ourselves, easily buffeted by harmful desires, and readily drawn from life to death. Let the very act of praise itself be a turning back to Thee, and a means of grace.

We thank Thee that we were made in Thine image;
> that however slight the resemblance at times, there is in us that which tells us we belong to Thee.

We thank Thee that Thou hast pledged Thy care of us;
> that however needful we may be in any given circumstances, the eternal is our refuge and underneath are the everlasting arms.

We thank Thee that Thy grace is ever greater than our sin;
> that however dark our sense of failure and defeat, Thy pardoning word stands sure and Thy peace is nigh.

Remembering Thy goodness in all places of Thy dominion, we are moved to offer Thee our praise.

Through Jesus Christ our Lord.

II

We pray today for all who use the slackened pace of summer as a time to review their loyalties, assess the direction of their lives, and struggle with decisions of long-standing consequence:
> We think of young people caught between the desire to get a job and the yearning for further education;
> men and women nearing the middle years, trying to summon the courage to break with work they do not like in order to begin again at something else;
> aging couples wondering whether to hang on for yet another year in their homes and apartments, or opt for that final move to a retirement village;
> moon-struck couples needing to find out whether what they feel for one another is surface attraction or durable love;

those in their late teens and early twenties who feel curiously
drawn to the ministry of Christ, but look for yet another sign;
folks of every age who are determined at last to stop playing
church and want, perhaps for the first time ever, to reckon
seriously with the claims of Christ:
O Thou who art the soul's unfailing light, dispose our anxious
hearts to go or stay as Thou dost lead, undaunted by the cost.

Through Jesus Christ our Lord.

III

We wait before Thee, gracious Father, in need of correction and
encouragement, stimulation and assurance, a glimpse of the larger
vision and a new awareness of the near at hand:
where our expectations have expired, let the piercing notes of
yet another reveille rouse us from our sleep;
where we live too close to the shocks and surprises of the headlines of the day, lead us nearer to the heart of things lest we
forget whose world it is;
where the illness or death of another has dropped life's song
into a minor key, stand by us to strengthen and bless until the
shadows lift and the morning comes.

Give us, O God, an eye for beauty,
an ear for truth,
and a heart that hungers after Thee.

We offer these our prayers in faith, aware that Thou art just in all
Thy ways.

Through Jesus Christ our Lord. *Amen.*

I

We bring ourselves to attention in Thy presence, gracious Lord, as those who find in Thee the *whence* and *why* and *whither* of their life. Our flirtations and affairs with gods of our own making, and our attempts to find abiding satisfaction in the train of passing circumstance, leave us in the end all the more intent on knowing and loving Thee.

We acclaim the goodness that assigned us life and gave it to us wrapped in freedom;
> the wisdom that made us different from each other so that the needs of one might interlock with the resources of his neighbor, completing both;
> the providence that stays our folly in crisis moments when human judgment falters;
> the grace that refreshes like a spring rain when the burden of our sin is more than we can bear.

It is alike our duty and our joy to offer Thee our thanks, O God.

Through Jesus Christ our Lord. *Amen.*

II

O Thou whose love goes out in unabated fullness to all the sons of men, hear us as we pray for those in our society who undergo the pain of adjusting to the unfamiliar:
> those in hospital for the first time;
> those who are "breaking in" on a new job;
> the aged mother recently admitted as guest in a retirement home;
> parents responding to the discovery of a son or daughter on drugs;
> the recently divorced;
> the recently bereaved;
> the recently paroled;
> the recently convicted.

O Thou who abidest the same above the changes and chances of our hurrying years, be near to all who need Thee as they brave the new; and let the comfort, pardon and direction of Thy good news in Christ meet them and lead them on.

Through Jesus Christ our Lord.

III

O God, the hope of all who seek Thee and the joy of all who find, move in our hearts who gather now before Thee.
Some of us are low and need the lifting word.
Some of us are high and need to be deflated.
Some of us are angry with the world.
Some not angry enough.
Some of us are certain about too much.
Some certain about too little.
O Thou who knowest every man for what he is and what he might become, bless each with what he needs the most, to the end that together we might better do Thy bidding.

All which we pray, grateful for a Saviour's love,
through Jesus Christ our Lord. *Amen.*

I

O God, there are blessings that come to us so clearly marked that even in our most disgruntled mood they compel our thanks.
But gathered now before Thee we would reflect on mercies that have come to us disguised, or reached us in roundabout ways:
We think of an unwelcome illness that shifted the center of our trust from self to Thee;
of new people who entered our life without our willing or wanting, and in time expanded our horizons and made us the better for their friendship;
of some prize that toppled from our grasp as we strained to reach it, causing us to change course and in the changing to discover life itself.
We remember long nights of heavy-hanging doubt that issued in a wiser, sturdier faith;
explosive arguments that aired differences, routed sham, located issues, and made authentic meeting possible;
challenges to our power that deflated the ego and left us with a humbler estimate of self.
For these and other back-door mercies, we give Thee thanks, dear God.

Through Jesus Christ our Lord.

II

O Thou whose will it is that men should pray and not faint, hear us as we pray for those who are finding life too much:
those who seem consigned to live on the ragged edge of poverty;
those for whom Thy name is a word on a coin, who have never heard that Thou art love, or seen that love in those about them;
men who have paid too much for their success and yearn to recover a soul lost along the way;
young people who feel themselves slipping ever deeper into a dependence on drugs and lack the will to extricate themselves;

those who are expected to be what they are not;
those who prefer to live at 33⅓ RPMs but find history spinning
    toward them at a dizzying 78.
O God, the strength of all who seek Thee out in every generation,
turn our fearful hearts to Thee, that we may stand as those whose
moorings are secure.

Through Jesus Christ our Lord.

III

Hear us now, gracious Father, as we petition Thee for light and
guidance for our church:
   We thank Thee for the diversity and commitment present in our
      ranks, for the willingness to work and the desire to be faith-
      ful to a trust;
   Save us from easy goals and cautious expectations, that we may
      stretch and reach and press to do what we attempt for Thee
      not somehow, but triumphantly!
   So replenish us, O God, that we may be a source of nourishment
      to others.
   So certify Thy love to us that we may live above the need for
      praise or the fear of criticism.
   Help us to live as those who have seen Thy glory in the face of
      Jesus Christ. And may that vision be our strength until life's
      day is ended and our work is done.

Through Jesus Christ our Lord.   *Amen.*

I

Our fathers trusted Thee, O God, and we would have our children trust Thee. For the only life we know is the life we have in Thee.

For the good earth, rich in mineral wealth and resplendent in beauty;

For the ties of blood and memory and tradition that link the passing generations to each other;

For the signs and gestures of love that work their magic in our hearts and keep us from becoming like the machines we operate;

For the sheer excitement of being present at this point in history when what is vital in the old struggles to connect with what is needed in the new:

Thy name be praised.

Through the action of Thy Spirit in our souls may the wonder of life and the joy of Thy salvation keep a song upon our lips, even a song of praise to Thee.

Through Jesus Christ our Lord.

II

We pray today for all who work to bring Thy healing to the sick:

doctors, nurses and technicians;

harassed hospital administrators;

members of hospital boards;

orderlies and kitchen help;

dependable volunteers;

and thoughtful neighbors.

O Thou who didst send Thy Son among us as a great physician, grant that the Spirit of Jesus may govern all who touch our sick in any way.

May the strength of our nation be found in generous provisions made for those who have suffered impairment of mind or body.

Let those of us who are strong bear the infirmities of the weak, and thus fulfill the law of Christ.

Through Jesus Christ our Lord.

III

We pray, finally, for ourselves, so varied in our needs that no one prayer can say it all.

Some of us are in a hurry, wanting the big prize now and we find ourselves on a local making every stop.

Some of us are reeling from a recent loss or relocation, and what was rock beneath our feet has turned to sand.

Some of us are suffering from flagging self-esteem, for those who knew us in our prime and remembered, keep moving on.

Some of us are trying to rope a bucking conscience, for we find we can neither hate those whom we are expected to hate nor love those whom we are called upon to love.

O God, for such as we is Thy grace given, without measure and without price. Humble us to receive Thy grace, and make us glad that we can never go where Thou art not, nor sink beneath the level of Thy love.

All which we pray,
      through Jesus Christ our Lord.   *Amen.*

I

Lord, we have the cares.

Our verve has been sapped by problems that keep coming at us for which we have no answers.

We know joy only as a "sometime thing," for most of our waking hours are anxiously strung together.

We live with a sense that all that we once prized is being inexorably diminished.

And our hearts are heavy.

O Thou who art never nearer to Thine own than when their systems quake and their idols fall;

Make us thankful that our ways are known to Thee:

that faith outlasts the night;

that Thy judgments are redemptive;

and Thy mercies sure.

Help us to rest in the joy of what Thou art, and to work in the happy confidence that the love we have met in Jesus Christ will some day rule the world.

So shall we have unfailing cause to bless Thy name.

Through Jesus Christ our Lord.

I I

Lord, in our prayers of intercession we would remember the in-between people, the middle-aged of our society, those men and women on whom the weight of responsibility falls most heavily:

too old to be fired by the visions of their youth,

too young to enjoy the slackened pace of those who are winding down,

concerned alike for aging parents and growing children,

hard-pressed financially,

highly taxed,

resentful of greying hair, softening muscles, reduced agility and lost youthfulness,

stung by the remorse of unfulfilled intentions,
disillusioned by the emptiness of goals already reached.

Minister to them, O God, out of Thine infinite power to bless.
Protect them against the destruction that wastes at noon, and the
fatigue that dogs the middle years. As the outer nature alters and
time takes its toll, let the inner man be renewed each day after the
working of Thine ageless and eternal Spirit.

Through Jesus Christ our Lord.

III

Our prayers are faint, O God, because our faith is weak.
Strengthen us in the same lest our religion be in word and form
alone, and not in power. Let that mind be in us which was in our
Saviour, that relationships may matter more to us than possessions,
and the Kingdom of God count for more than the kingdoms of this
world.
Give us sight to see our sins, the grace to confess them, the will to
forsake them, and the wisdom to learn from them, that we may
grow into the likeness of Christ, more faithfully to do Thy will.

Through Jesus Christ our Lord. *Amen.*

I

O Thou who art the hope of all who seek Thee, and the joy of all who find; even on our darkest days we have cause to praise Thy name:

> that there should be a universe at all;
>
> that we should be granted the incredible miracle of life;
>
> that we should be able to perceive purpose and design, notice beauty, feel and communicate joy;
>
> that we should know ourselves free and responsible;
>
> that we should be upheld by a love we often spurn, and over-tured again and again by a spirit we frequently resist;
>
> that there is healing for our hurts, comfort for our sorrows, light for our darkness, and pardon for our sins.

O Lord, our Lord, how excellent is Thy name in all the earth. Take to Thyself the thanks we raise to Thee.

Through Jesus Christ our Lord.

II

Here in this house of prayer we would pray for all who are fast becoming slaves of unworthy masters:

> those who are leaning more and more on the glass crutch of alcohol;
>
> those whose style of life is increasingly controlled by peer group pressures;
>
> those whose daily work kills the soul inch by inch;
>
> those for whom money has passed from a means to an end;
>
> those who have become so dependent on order that they can only curse the new, and fear it;
>
> those who are formally committed to loyalties they no longer feel;
>
> those in public office who find their political debts stifling their ability to say and do what's right.

O thou who art more willing to set us free than we are to walk
in freedom, show us Thy love and in Thy mercy save us.

Through Jesus Christ our Lord.   *Amen.*

III

Lord, in the quiet of this hour before Thee, we would pause to ask
for a surer knowledge of who we are and what we are about.
  If we can recall a time when we loved Thee more, restore.
  If we have become good friends with some favorite sin, rebuke.
  If the flame of our commitment to the world's awful need flickers
    dimly, rekindle.
  If along the way a relationship once cherished stands endangered
    through some wrong, real or imagined, reunite.

Show us the relevance of Christ for the life we live within and
the world we make for others,
that we may no longer live to ourselves but unto Him whom we
call Saviour, Lord and Friend.

Through Jesus Christ our Lord.   *Amen.*

I

Eternal God, our Father, rich in mercy and lavish in Thy care of us. Thy great name be praised.

We thank Thee for blessings that meet the eye:
  the glow of good health;
  the welcome sight of a friend's face in a large crowd;
  the carefree laughter of children at play;
  the taste of well-cooked food;
  the beauty of the sky on a star-filled night.

We thank Thee even more for blessings that are felt but never seen:
  Thy peace at work in our hearts;
  invisible ties of faith that bind together all who love the Lord;
  courage that courses through our being when danger beckons;
  stamina that keeps us "at it" even when we don't feel like it;
  confidence in the Kingdom of God that saves us from prolonged
    doubt and shields us from despair;
  our vulnerability to the memory of kindnesses done us by friends
    and loved ones over the years.

Fearfully and wonderfully made, we are graciously kept and furnished. We acknowledge and acclaim Thy goodness to us.

Through Jesus Christ our Lord.

II

We pray today, gracious Father, for all who are hard put to come to terms with time:
  the young, for whom time seems to go so slowly;
  the middle-aged who find themselves with too little time to do
    all the things they wish;
  the elderly, who mourn the irreversibility of time and live with
    a frantic sense that almost all the sand has dropped.
We pray for those who can only think to "kill" time:

those with vengeance in their hearts, who are carefully biding
   time;
those who are immobilized by indecision, and nervously mark
   time;
those in penal institutions, who are doing time;
those who will not age gracefully, and spend much wealth and
   energy resisting time;
those who cannot reconcile the eternal Christ to the tragedies
   and ambiguities of time.

O Thou who hast set eternity in our hearts, yet given us to live by
clocks and calendars, help us to see our years as a hallowed trust,
and Thy Kingdom and its righteousness as the end toward which
we move.

Through Jesus Christ our Lord.

III

Too proud to cry, O God,
Often too grim to laugh,
Too sophisticated to enjoy,
Often too hard to repent,
We bow before Thee now to pray for ourselves.

Each of us is known to Thee and loved by Thee, as if there were
no other. Help us, then, to see ourselves for the children of God
we are:
   let the beauty of Jesus win us to a new affection for all that
      builds life up;
   let the suffering of Jesus make us patient toward those who
      mean us harm;
   let the presence of Jesus endow us with poise, however fierce
      the pressure;
   let the power of Jesus confirm in us the hope that while sorrow
      endures for a night, joy comes in the morning.

We pray from the heart, and in the spirit of thanksgiving,
   through Jesus Christ our Lord.   *Amen.*

I

For reasons that we do not altogether understand, O God, it is easier for us to find fault than to give thanks. Our grievances lie on the tip of our tongue, while mercies that ought to excite our praise are easily lost from view.
We thank Thee for truth and the varied forms in which it comes to us:
    in closely reasoned logic,
    in scientific demonstrations,
    in the forceful impact of a well-staged drama,
    in inspired verse,
    in the brilliance of a painted masterpiece,
    in the shattering disclosures of Scripture,
    in the self-sight that comes from a shared love,
    in the clarifying ecstasy of prayer and meditation.

O Thou who art the author of all truth, help us in our search to find the same. By the quiet action of Thy Holy Spirit in our hearts lead us at last or again to Jesus, that in His presence we may know:
    who we are,
    and whose we are,
    and why we are.
Then, with a confidence born of faith, we shall have yet one cause more for which to bless Thy Name.

Through Jesus Christ our Lord.

II

We join our prayers today in intercession for men and women in our society who are trapped:
    those who are trapped in poverty with no sign of relief;
    those who are trapped in jobs that engage but a fraction of their
      powers;

those who are trapped in families where love has ebbed away;
those who are trapped in unwanted alliances out of which they
  cannot break;
those who are trapped by the fear of discovery, or by dependency
  on others, or by a need for drugs, or by an addiction to al-
  cohol.

O Thou whose will it is that we be free, and who didst give Thy
Son that we might be delivered from all coercive powers:
  make us examples of Thy freedom, proclaimers of Thy freedom,
    and instruments of Thy freedom;
  snap our chains that we may loose the chains of others.
Then shall the joy of the liberated rise from the earth like a mighty
hymn of praise.

Through Jesus Christ our Lord.

III

Confident of Thy care, we pray now for ourselves.
We are many things to many people, but in Thy sight Thy sons
and daughters.
  Encourage us in obedience where we have grown lax.
  Restore us in tenderness where we have grown hard.
  Renew us in purpose where we have grown confused.
Uphold the bereaved in their loneliness, and give our sick to know
that Thine ear is not heavy that it cannot hear, nor Thine arm short
that it cannot save. Bless us, each one, with an unhindered view of
Thy majesty that, sure of the power at work within us, we may live,
not somehow, but triumphantly.

Through Jesus Christ our Lord. *Amen.*

AMONG YOU AS ONE WHO SERVES

Let wrong embolden us to fight,
and need excite our care;
If not us, who? If not now, when?
If not here, God, then where?

I

Almighty God, Creator of the world in which we live and builder of the church through which we serve, it is good and altogether right, whatever our mood or station, that we should praise Thy name.

We thank Thee for words of encouragement that find us when our flame is low;
>   for helpful hands that reach us when the load is more than we can bear;
>   for retrievable insights that come to mind when two ways open and we must decide.
> Nor would we fail to thank Thee for Thy governance and love,
>   and for all who by word and life and dependence on Thy spirit have brought our doubting souls to faith.

We remember with gratitude the founding pastor of this church,
>   the scope of his agile mind,
>   the vision that commanded him,
>   and the lives he touched across the years of a long and fruitful life.
Help us to continue what he so well began, and to Thy name be praise.

Through Jesus Christ our Lord.

II

We remember before Thee today the laymen of Thy church whose witness to Thee is largely made beyond these walls. We thank Thee,
>   for Christian teachers, Christian lawyers, Christian businessmen;
>   for Christians in politics, Christians in building construction and maintenance, Christians in the arts, and
>   for Christians in the home.

Bless them with a sense of Thy presence on the job, to the end that they may do their work well, and in the doing of it be a Christ to those around them.

Forgive us that our influence has never matched our numbers;
    that we have spent more time enjoying our faith than applying it;
    that so many of our friends have no idea at all of what Christ
      means to us.
Where others drift, help us to move with purpose;
Where others doubt, help us to believe;
Where others despair, help us to hope in Thee.

Through Jesus Christ our Lord.

III

O Thou searcher of all hearts, in whose sight the fine print of our private history is as a billboard, whatever else we may lack in our worship, let us at least be as honest as we can.
    Deliver us from the need to build ourselves up by cutting others
      down.
    Free us from the pride that makes acknowledgment of wrong
      difficult.
    Give us the grace to back away from earlier positions with the
      coming of fresh light.
    Keep us at peace in the center of our being, however turbulent
      the causes we support.

Let Thy comfort enfold every grieving heart among us.
The stout promises of Thy Holy Word embolden all who are afraid;
And Thy judgments shake the lethargy of all who are at ease in
    Zion.

Through Jesus Christ our Lord. *Amen.*

I

Almighty God, forgive us the turn of mind that makes us look on our abundance as a matter of right rather than an evidence of grace.

We thank Thee for our breath and bread;
    for a universe soundly made;
    for man's ability to remember and his capacity for hope.

We thank Thee for serious minds that grapple with tall questions while the rest go on with their games; for jovial souls who lubricate the mechanisms of society with a saving sense of humor.

We thank Thee for a book that reads us;
    for a church in which the strong bear the infirmities of the weak;
    for sacraments that tell of a pledged love;
    for a garden, a cross, and an empty tomb.

For this and so much more we thank Thee and bless Thy name, through Jesus Christ our Lord.

II

Hear us now as we pray for Thy church, Catholic and Apostolic:
    Bless it with sound scholarship, lest it be tempted to fill an intellectual gap with devotional material;
    Bless it with the poise that belongs to faith, lest in rushing to be relevant it should become irrelevant to the gospel;
    Bless it with person-centeredness, lest stones and statistics, size and structure, come to mean too much.
    Bless it with the willingness to learn, lest it succumb to the arrogance of knowing all of the answers and none of the questions.
    Bless it with a new confidence in prayer, lest it fail both man and Thee through withheld supplication.

Raise up men and women who will love and serve the church in the fullness of their powers.

Through Jesus Christ our Lord.

III

We pray now for all who are joined in this experience of worship, together in this place or in solitude beside a radio. Whatever else we may or may not be, O God, make us honest in Thy sight:
Honest to admit our fears and sins;
Honest to concede that we have twisted fact to suit our purpose;
Honest to acknowledge the masks we use to keep the inner self concealed;
Honest to confess that we are often secretly drawn to the things we openly decry.

O Thou who art the author of grace and truth, incline our hearts toward Thee that we may know Thy peace,
And to Thy name be praise from us and from all men,
And from Thy saints who serve Thee in the courts above.

Through Jesus Christ our Lord.   *Amen.*

I

O Thou who art the author of life, the end towards which the whole creation moves, and yet withal our Father; hear us as we praise and magnify Thy name:
>We fancy ourselves a self-made people;
>>we are in fact contingent, dependent, and derived.
>We fancy ourselves a reasonable people;
>>we are in fact beset with blind spots, and all too often conscript our minds in the service of our prejudices.
>We fancy ourselves free;
>>we are in fact in bondage to our flesh and to material possessions that we chase with much abandon.
>We fancy ourselves fully alive;
>>we are in fact but dimly aware of the heights and depths, the breadth and length, the wonder and miracle of life, there for our exploring.
>We fancy ourselves decent and religious;
>>we are in fact continually falling short of our potential and prone to use our faith to justify a selfish use of life.

That Thou shouldst love us, when we find it hard to love ourselves;
That Thou shouldst believe in us, after we have blown so many chances;
That Thou shouldst welcome us, when we can bring so little;
Is more than we can understand.
>But we can accept Thy love,
>>bless Thee for Thy grace,
>And voice our thanks to Thee;
>>which now we do together.

Through Jesus Christ our Lord.

II

O Thou who desirest justice in the earth, hear us as we pray for all who work to right wrong, and champion the cause of the oppressed.

Especially do we pray for those within that company who weary in the struggle and are tempted to step down:

> We acknowledge, Lord, a preference for quick and easy answers. We like our instant coffee, instant credit, instant news, and inwardly we pine for instant resolution of the ills that plague our world.
>
> Hold to their high purpose those who would be faithful to the vision despite the pressures of apathy and antagonism.
>
> Renew the strength of those who work long and sleep little day after day, prodding this nation to become to all its citizens what it has been to some.

O God, help us to learn from Thee, who art never in a hurry, yet never late. Bless us with Thy poise, Thy persistence, and Thy peace.

Through Jesus Christ our Lord.

III

Hear us, gracious Father, as we pray for this church: its mission, its ministers, its people. Bless us individually and together with an immediate experience of Thy power, to the end that the fire within our hearts may vitalize our worship and energize our work.

> For the sick, we ask Thy healing touch.
> For the lonely, Thy companionship.
> For the weak, Thy strength.
> For the undecided, Thy wisdom.
> For the bereaved, Thy comfort.

Melt our indifference toward each other;

> help us to see Thy face in our neighbor's countenance;
> and to love him in Thee, and for Thee.

We pray in faith and with thanksgiving,

> through Jesus Christ our Lord. *Amen.*

I

We thank Thee, God, for life and light and all things good:
for home and work and play;
for time's ability to heal old wounds;
for friends in whose affection we find a sense of worth and purpose.

Against all that would crush it, we thank Thee that we still believe in the kingdom that Jesus saw,
and taught,
and died for;
that even in those stretches when it would appear that chaos triumphs over us we keep discovering clues that point to Thee.

For modest victories over sin;
For the power of the Scriptures over us;
For the church, not yet without its spots and wrinkles;
And chiefly for Thyself, our Saviour, Lord and King:
we bless Thy Holy name.

Through Jesus Christ our Lord.

I I

We pray today for Thy church, widely scattered over all the earth, shaken by the winds of change, yet wanting in its heart to speak the word that matters and do the thing that counts.

Help Thy church, O God, to be patient with itself; lest the biting acids of untempered criticism eat away the loyalty of her finest sons and daughters.

Help Thy church, O God, to know what is negotiable and what is not; lest its worship be stripped of the transcendent, its gospel be reduced to a set of rationally validated principles, and its witness in society be nothing more than a prayed-over version of the rigid right or the raucous left.

Help Thy church, O God, to live in close connection with the
sources of its power; lest a reliance on public relations tech-
niques, an obsession with statistics, and a tendency to fear
for its own life should curb the provocative and comforting
action of Thy Holy Spirit.
Make Thy church, O God, what it was meant to be: beginning
with us.

Through Jesus Christ our Lord.

III

Such is the nature of our life, O God, and so sorely have we been
deceived, that we can go for days, weeks, months, even years, without an honest prayer.

Sealing ourselves off against mystery;
Relying heavily on native wit and acquired skills;
Postponing life's big questions;
Staying busy getting and spending:
    we have a way of making Thee, our God, an expendable extra.
Move into our lives, O God, in a saving, centering way, confirming
    what is strong in us and filling what is empty.
Let Thy love so possess us that whatever we do in word or deed
we may do in Thy strength, and mindful of Thy glory.

Through Jesus Christ our Lord.   *Amen.*

I

Gracious God our Father, beneath whose eye and within whose patience the story of our years is told, compose us in Thy presence and help us to pray more nearly as we ought.

We thank Thee for our names, and those who know us by them:
For skills of mind or hand that render us employable;
For folks about us who care what we think and how we feel;
For invisible forces, like memory and hope, encouragement and praise, that enhance the gift of life and stretch us to greater effort.

We thank Thee for the very gift of faith that prompts our prayers:
For those who conveyed it to us;
For life experiences that tested and confirmed it;
For the living Christ whose presence in the world and in our hearts makes it all worthwhile.

Our praise, spoken and unspoken, we offer gladly now to Thee, through Jesus Christ our Lord.

II

We unite our hearts to pray for Thy church, O God:
scattered across the face of all the earth; under attack by critics from without;
riddled by dissension and faithlessness within;
here, too quick to scuttle ancient ways;
there, too prone to cling to outworn practice;
and yet, withal, Thy church.
Grant to Thy body a fresh doubt-scattering confidence in Jesus Christ its head:
an ability to dream dreams, and the will to work to bring those dreams to pass;

the power to challenge evil rather than accept it, and the willingness to pass from words to actual caring for the bent and
broken, the careless and listless casualties of earth.
Let Thy drumbeat sound in the hearts of those who bear Thy name,
and bid Thy people "March."

Through Jesus Christ our Lord.

III

We look now to our own needs, and the wants that masquerade
as needs; and pray for the wisdom to know one from the other:
Help us to accept ourselves, that we may be delivered from the
need for self-promotion;
Help us to commit ourselves, that we may shake the need to be
diverted and distracted;
Help us to deny ourselves, that the strident clamorings of the
flesh and self may be subdued;
Help us to know ourselves, that we may neither overestimate
nor underestimate our gifts;
Let Thy love so prevail in the life and ministry of this congregation that each may count the other precious, and all of us
together erect within these walls, and beyond, a testimony to
the truth that sets men free.

We pray to Thee, O Father, in the power of the Spirit.

Through Jesus Christ our Lord. *Amen.*

I

O Thou who art the source of all things good, grant that we who are inclined to remember what we lack may not forget what we have.

> We bless Thee for the warming quality of spring: for lengthened days, green grass, budding flowers, and all the scents and colors that edge us into summer.

> We thank Thee for the interflow of ideas, the sharing of convictions, man's ability to receive and infuse hope, and the play of divine truth on the human spirit.

> Our highest praise we reserve for Thee, our God, whose mercy is the same from age to age, and whose life-giving grace has been declared and pledged to us in Jesus Christ.

Center our far-ranging lives in Thine eternal love, that in whatever time or circumstance we may know and celebrate Thy presence.

Through Jesus Christ our Lord.

II

O Thou who hast made clear our duty to pray for one another, hear us now as we pray for those servants of the cross who work in hard and trying places:

> chaplains in the Armed Forces who break the bread of life to troubled men and women;

> pastors in congregations that are beset by shrinking funds, narrow-mindedness, and a paralyzing fear of change;

> fraternal workers in distant lands whose ministries are closely watched by hostile governments;

> social workers in our major cities who carry on their hearts the burden of the poor, and attempt a ministry of hope against oppressive odds;

> men and women in public life who strive to effect sorely needed change within the complicated maze of politics;

> Insightful journalists who use the printed word to expose our idols and blast us out of our ruts.

Grant to all (such,) Heavenly Father, the stamina to stay with it.
And show us, (whose ways are less demanding,) how we may give
them of our strength, and uphold them in their work.

Through Jesus Christ our Lord.

III

Come near to us, each one, O Lord, for behind the front that we
struggle to maintain there lurks a self that is frequently—
   doubtful of its ends,
   unsure of its worth,
   unhappy with its prospects,
   and annoyed with its limitations.

Make real in us the life that Jesus came to bring, lest the cares
either of self or society rob us of the joy of being human.
Anxious though we are about the long view, help us to take the
step immediately before us, knowing that of such the story of our
life is made.

Keep us true to our best insights, all the way, to the very end.

Through Jesus Christ our Lord. *Amen.*

I

Our Father and our God—because we can only learn to pray by praying—we dare to bring Thee now our prayers, unfinished as they are.

We give Thee unbounded thanks for forces at work around us and within which keep us from resigning ourselves to that which ought to be resisted:

> for the unrest of the young, and their vision of a world unblighted by war and exploitation;
>
> for city planners and their dreams for a metropolis void of ghettoes and adorned with beauty;
>
> for conservationists who quicken our imagination with pictures of a world in which the gentle balances of nature are preserved, wherein the air is clean and the water unpolluted;
>
> for voices, lonely and prophetic, that call us to a new earth, a new humanity, and a new church.

We thank Thee for friends who take us as we are and gently urge us on to better things. And for Thy Holy Spirit who gives us to see the interim character of the little systems in which we take such pride.

Lead on, O King Eternal, and give us faith to follow.

Through Jesus Christ our Lord.

II

Hear us now as we pray for those who practice the ministry of translation:

> those who translate into our mother tongue the works of other lands and languages;
>
> those who translate a mystical communion with Thee into courageous moral action;
>
> those who translate a technical knowledge of the workings of the human mind into helpful therapy;

those who translate their grasp of complex issues into programs
that work for the healing of the nations;

those who translate the wisdom of the past into guidelines for
the present;

those who translate their faith in God into little nameless, un-
remembered acts of kindness and of love.

Swell their ranks, O God, and help them to rise above the indifference and ingratitude that so often greet their work.

Through Jesus Christ our Lord.

III

Out of Thine infinite love, O God, minister to us in our several
needs. Give us mastery over moodiness and petulance,

the ability to smile even on the worst of days,

the stamina to persevere when the prize eludes our grasp,

the courage to resume life alone when parted from a friend of
many years,

the faith to believe that a grand design exists even when we cannot see it,

the grace to acknowledge guilt and the humility to accept forgiveness.

And all to Thine eternal praise.

Through Jesus Christ our Lord. *Amen.*

I

Lord, there are times when all that keeps our faith afloat is a sense of gratitude toward Thee. The headlines of the day beat us down, and evil within us and about us lays us open to paralyzing doubt. Then we recall Thy gifts of nature and of grace, and in that recalling find power to go on.

We thank Thee for reason and affection; for our unity with everything that lives and breathes; for poetry that utters what the heart holds; for friendships of long standing that multiply our joys and temper our disappointments.

We thank Thee most that we live in dialogue with Thee; that we have proved prayer real and known the strength of supporting love in our seasons of defeat.

It is good that men should praise Thy name, and we would do it now.

Through Jesus Christ our Lord.

I I

O Thou who hast willed a variety of gifts in the one body of Thy church,

hear us as we pray for a more productive fusion of insights and abilities among Thy people;

guard us against wasteful rivalries and unwarranted divisions to the end that each may rejoice in the gifts and talents of the other;

in particular, we pray that clergy and laymen may march together as beneath one banner in the spirit of mutual trust and interdependence.

Whatever the nature of our work, help us, O God, to do it unto Thee.

Let our shops and offices, our schools and factories, our streets and homes, feel the influence of Christ through us.

Use our assorted skills and aptitudes in the manner of a con-
ductor with his orchestra, calling out this instrument, then
that; this section, then another, to offer their best in a grand
performance of the work at hand. Tune us to Thy will and
harmonize us with each other and with Thee.

Through Jesus Christ our Lord.

III

Some of us, Lord, are troubled and need the comforts and con-
solations of the gospel; some of us are living in a dream world of
relative ease and tranquillity and need to be called to attention
again by a disconcerting word from beyond.

Fashion Thy coming according to the present status of our
hearts, but visit us again, we beseech Thee.

Renew our love for the Scriptures, our hunger for meaningful
relationships, our discontent with mediocrity, our willingness
to contend for the right, our readiness to claim our limitations.

For we would make our years count, and advance Thy glory in
the earth.

Through Jesus Christ our Lord. *Amen.*

I

Most merciful and gracious Father, forgive us that in our money-centered culture we so easily develop the acquisitive spirit at the cost of a thankful heart. Stir our memories lest praise be thwarted by a failure to recall Thy goodness.

We thank Thee for blessings that come to us clearly marked as such:
    sumptuous food, good health, clear minds,
    deliverance from danger, abiding friendships,
    the unspeakable gift of Thy salvation.
But we would thank Thee, too, for blessings that come to us disguised:
    temporary setbacks that work a more enduring good;
    unwelcome burdens that make us stronger for their weight;
    sieges of illness that destroy our notions of indispensability;
    confrontation with disturbing points of view that cause us to
        check our own position and earn the ground we hold;
    soul-deep feelings of guilt and loneliness which serve as prods to
        get us out of the far country and back to the Father's house.
Grant us, O God, the faith to see Thee as Thou art, that we may praise Thee as we ought.

Through Jesus Christ our Lord.

II

Hear us, O Lord, as we pray for the Holy Catholic Church, Thy Church:
    proclaiming a better gospel than it has ever lived;
    panicked by the boisterous winds of change that whistle through
        its courts;
    aping the world in its dependence on wealth and pretentious
        buildings, invoking the skills of Madison Avenue to sell the
        Via Dolorosa;
    ashamed at times of its beginnings: the cup, the Cross, the towel;
    and yet withal the community of grace, loved and kept by Thee.

Give to Thy Church, O Lord, the courage that comes from knowing that Christ means to win that for which He died:
    the faith that comes with the hearing of Thy Word;
    the commitment to service that is born and nourished in com-
        munion with Thee;
    the quality of life that comes when the cost of discipleship is
        declared and the strong rise up to answer, "Yes."

Revive Thy Church, O God.
Revive Thy Church through us, we pray.

Through Jesus Christ our Lord.

III

We pray now, Father, for our needs, insofar as we can distinguish
what we need from what we want:
    We want friends; we need deliverance from overweening pride
        that puts others off.
    We want light; we need discipline to sustain the search for truth.
    We want peace; we need patience for that which makes for
        peace.
    We want excitement; we need victory over drugs and artificial
        stimulants, and the courage to face life as it is.
    We want love; we need fidelity, the only context in which au-
        thentic love can flourish.

Destroy what is evil in us, O God, and incline our hearts toward
good.

All which we dare to pray,
    through Jesus Christ our Lord. *Amen.*

I

Lord, we have been taught that to survive in the city we must keep our feelings to ourselves, play it cool, never talk to strangers, cherish privacy, and honor the formalities that provide protective distance between ourselves and other people.

All the more reason, then, why we should thank Thee for friends and acquaintances,
    authors and playwrights,
    artists and musicians,
who have countered convention and dared to express themselves. Through their initiative we have gotten off dead center and inched a little closer toward knowing who we are.

Most of all we thank Thee for Thy self-disclosure in Jesus of Nazareth;
    that in Him we see Thy will convincingly revealed;
    and through Him feel the love that from of old has gone out
      from Thy heart for all the sons of men.

Thy name, O God, be praised.
Through Jesus Christ our Lord.

I I

We pray, Lord, for Thy church, scattered far and wide:
    clinging to old ways in a new day, or else rushing to embrace the
      new in reckless abandon of the past;
    here suffering from battle fatigue, there afflicted with inertia;
    at times embarrassed by its Galilean accent, at other times so
      thoroughly assimilated to the surrounding culture as to lose all
      distinctiveness;
    in some instances foolishly competitive, in others superficially
      merged around harmless affirmations;
    often given to deeds uninterpreted by words, more often given
      to words unaffirmed by action.

Bless Thy church, O God, with divine guidance and direction,
that in the thick of life,
and at those points where men are hurting,
we may be Thy servant people.

Through Jesus Christ our Lord.

III

Here in this our house of prayer, we would pause to pray for ourselves:
Down inside some of us carry a brokenness too deep for telling;
Some of us are madly in love with a past that can never be again;
Many of us are tired trying to sustain the image of a self that no longer exists;
Not a few of us have grown hard and unmannerly from battling social wrongs, and we want to be civil again;
Others of our number have become worldly-wise and sophisticated at the expense of neglected prayer and a seldom-opened Bible, and we yearn to feel that oneness with Thee which marked our earlier years.
O Thou whose name we bear,
Thou hast loved us, love us still;
until our conflicts are resolved,
our imbalances are corrected,
and our sins, which are many, lose their appeal for us before the beauty of Thy righteousness.

All which we pray in faith and with thanksgiving,
through Jesus Christ our Lord. *Amen.*

AROUND THE CHRISTIAN YEAR

Our people move with downcast eyes,
  tight, sullen and afraid;
Surprise us with Thy joy divine,
  for we would be remade.

Advent

I

Lord, that we are alive,
  that food is delicious to the taste,
  that the ground is firm beneath our tread,
  that rest can compensate for toil,
  that earth might be fair and all her sons be blest,
Thy name be praised.

We thank Thee for friends who care,
  for ways that open when every door seems shut,
  for the reality of forgiveness—human and divine,
  for major purposes that make life's minor irritations bearable,
  for the confidence that man's gravest ills will yield to sacrifice
    and toil.

We thank Thee for Thyself—ground and source of every good—
and especially for Thy love, that no resistance can diminish, and
no need exhaust.
With all Thy people in every corner of creation, we count it joy to
praise Thy name.

Through Jesus Christ our Lord.

I I

We pray today for those who are up against hard numbers:
  those in prison who serve a fixed sentence;
  those in hospital whose life expectancy is a matter of days;
  those who must make a payment on a note at a set time;
  those being forced to move to unfamiliar quarters, on a date
    already assigned;
  those who must retire from the only life they know on a day
    already circled in black;
  those who know that their income from work or welfare cannot
    meet their family needs;
  those who find a deadline staring them in the face as they
    agonize over a decision.

O Thou who art the Lord of Life, make us sensitive to those who feel such pressures, knowing that it is a matter of grace and not of merit that we are not there ourselves. And make man's extremity Thine opportunity to save.

Through Jesus Christ our Lord.

III

We dare now to pray for ourselves, ashamed that we have done so little with so much, yet struggling to offer Thee a more obedient service.

Give us keener self-understanding—as keen as we can bear at one sitting—lest we think of ourselves more highly, or lowly, than we ought.

Give us a sense of what is vital in life—lest we squander our years and waste our attention on inflated trifles.

Give us a due regard for our unity with all men lest we think in tribal patterns and forget that Thou art Lord of all the earth.

We ask, Lord, for ourselves the most meaningful Advent season we have ever known.

Drive us to our knees;
   to the Book;
   to an awareness of our sin;
   to a careful searching of our virtues;
   to a serious examination of words and terms so glibly sung and spoken.

Measure us, O God, according to Thy judgments, but take not Thy mercy from us.

And grant that when Christmas morning breaks for us this year, we may have something more to show for our much running about than tired feet, wrapped presents, and regrets for cards not sent.

When Thou saidst, "Seek ye my face," my heart said unto Thee, "Thy face, Lord, will I seek."

Through Jesus Christ our Lord. *Amen.*

Christmas

I

O God, our Father, whom we trust but do not fully understand; whom we love, but surely not with all our hearts; give us, we pray Thee, not the kind of Christmas we want, but the kind we need.
We live with a sense of crowdedness;
remind us of the providence that marks a sparrow's fall.
We live with a shrinking sense of personal worth;
remind us of a love to which each soul is precious.
We live with a sense of the years going by too quickly;
remind us of abiding purposes in which all that comes to pass partakes of the eternal.
We live with a sense of wrongs committed and good undone or unattempted;
remind us that for such the shepherd seeks, the Father waits.
Our souls take their rest, O God, in the joy of what Thou art. Let it be enough that Thou art for us, with us, and within us,
through Jesus Christ our Lord.

I I

O Thou who didst send Thy Son among us that the Word might be made flesh, bless with Thy favor and encouragement those in our time who would "flesh out" the Scriptures and make credible the Gospel to an unbelieving age:
All who earnestly work for peace;
All who deliberately live on less than they might in order to share with those who have less than they need;
All who make it their business to plead the cause of the orphan, the prisoner and the oppressed;
All who stand up in any company to challenge racial slurs and expose prejudice;
All who have trained themselves to listen with genuine concern to those who need an outlet for their grievances and cares;
All who have gone to the trouble of learning the Gospel well enough to be able to share it with others.

O Thou who hast told us clearly in the drama of Bethlehem that words alone won't do, help us productively to couple what we say with what we are and do, lest our rhetoric outrun our deeds,
   through Jesus Christ our Lord.

III

O Thou who hast chosen the weak things of earth to confound the mighty:
   Give us, Thy people, so susceptible to size, so easily impressed by worldly rank and scope; give us, O God, an eye for mangers tucked away in stables, and an ear for truth whose only fanfare is the rippled intuitions of the heart.
   Visit our sick with quiet assurance of Thy care.
   Encircle the bereaved with Thy warming, healing presence.
   Point out markers on the trail for those who have lost their way.
   And douse with the cold waters of common sense any who might this very day be on the verge of some destructive action or decision.
The race is short, O God, even at its longest, and we would run it well, and to Thy glory.

Through Jesus Christ our Lord. *Amen.*

Ash Wednesday

I

Eternal God, our Father, praise be to Thee for Thine unwavering goodness to the sons of men:
    for mercies that fall like rain on the just and the unjust;
    for words that find us in our seasons of not-knowing;
    for songs Thy love has taught our hearts to sing;
    for coincidental happenings which, viewed in retrospect, bespeak
      Thy gentle leading and Thy care;
    for good memories and true hopes, and every thought of Thee.

II

We commend to Thee this night those who stand in special need of prayer:
    all whose souls are hammered daily on the anvils of prejudice,
      and those who have broken with established social patterns
      to give them help;
    all who are aged and enfeebled, and those who hover round them
      like ministering angels;
    all who are retarded in mind or handicapped in body, and those
      who have taken their plight to heart and resolved to do them
      good;
    all whose lives are twisted by fear and superstition, and those
      who have gone to share with them the healing light of Christ.

III

For ourselves, O God, we find it hard to pray.
Well-clothed, well-housed, well-fed, well-served by gadgets and conveniences, what lack we yet?

O Thou who art holy beyond our telling, with whom we dare not trifle:
    show us our poverty of spirit and the leanness of our souls;
    give us the will to search out new definitions of self-denial;

teach our untaught hearts to love with a love like unto Thine;
curb our sloth;
expose the timidity and unbelief that lie behind our craving for
    security;
give us—in these days—to know, as we have not yet known,
    Jesus Christ in the power of His resurrection and the fellow-
    ship of His suffering.

These mercies we seek in faith, and with thanksgiving, in His
name. *Amen.*

Passion Sunday

I

O Lord, our Lord, how excellent is Thy name in all the earth. One age declares Thy goodness to another, and Thy steadfast love is the mainstay of our ever-restless hearts.

We thank Thee for the mystery of our years and the will to live;
　　for the rewards of solitude and the pleasure of congenial company;
　　for satisfactions that follow work well done, and the renewing power of leisure.
We thank Thee for hard choices that help us discover who we are;
　　for goodwill from unexpected sources that finds us in our seasons of depression;
　　and for the gift of faith that makes Thy love in Christ the broad and sure foundation on which we build.
Unashamed and unrestrained, we offer Thee the tribute of our thanks,
　　through Jesus Christ our Lord.

II

Bless with Thy power and presence, Gracious Father, those who do the menial chores and thankless tasks behind our city's bright façade:
　　Those who rise early to bring fresh food and produce from the marketplace;
　　Those who clean our halls and offices through the night;
　　Those who man our switchboards and see that messages get through;
　　Those who load and unload trucks;
　　Those who stock the shelves and work the back rooms of our stores;
　　Those who fire boilers and provide maintenance in the heat and noise of basements that we seldom visit;

Those who clean our windows and mend our masonry and keep
    our flagpoles in repair;
Those who set tables, bus dishes and man our many kitchens.
In following our several callings, make us aware of what we owe
to unnamed thousands whose work is indispensable to our well-
being. And give them to know, O God, that in Thy sight, if not in
ours, the least of the earth are very big indeed,
    through Jesus Christ our Lord.

III

As we near the hallowed ground of Gethsemane and Golgotha, we
confess to a sense of unworthiness and shame.
    Our deprivations are so few;
    Our scars so scarce;
    Our courage so seldom summoned;
    Our passion so wasted on self;
Who are we that we should bear Thy name or purport to be Thy
people?

Forgive us, Father, for we know not what we do.
    Expose the gamesmanship we work on Thee to stave off the
        moment of full surrender;
    And help us to come as the sinners we are, that we may obtain
        mercy and find grace to help in time of need.

Our prayers we offer in faith and with thanksgiving,
    through Jesus Christ our Lord. *Amen.*

Palm Sunday

I

O Thou, who art our light and our salvation, the source of every good we know, and the ground of all our hope, give us, even in these problem-ridden days, the wit and will—and faith—to praise Thy Holy Name.

We thank Thee that Thou art ever knocking, pleading, bidding, calling, speaking to the sons of men out of a love that will not quit;
 that even our lean years come by reason of Thy care.
 The pangs of emptiness that accompany our getting what we want—what are they but signals that we have no home but Thee!

Loose the Hosannas that stick in our sophisticated throats.
Overrule the pride that makes us too rigid for a good parade.
Let the child in each of us come alive again that we may strew our well-pressed garments in the pathway of the King.

Tear us away from the mini-purposes that drain our blood and sweat, that our blinkered eyes may catch the splendor of that noble vision of Thy will that fed the soul of Christ, that it may be to us our meat and drink.
Bless the Lord, O my soul, and all that is within me, bless His Holy Name.

Through Jesus Christ our Lord.

I I

We pray today for all who find themselves at work at the pressure points of history, amid the swirl of controversy, coping with the ferment of the day under the kleig lights of unrelenting publicity:
 Heads of state,
 University presidents,
 Magistrates and judges,

Police commissioners,
School principals,
Civil rights workers,
Church executives,
Urban renewal experts,
and a host of others whose actions and decisions make them more
often the targets of our criticism than the subjects of our prayers.
Renew them from within.
Free them from the need of human praise.
Bless them with a sense of alliance with Thee and a keen eye
for truth.
Through them, and all who serve the common good, lead this
nation on to Thee, and the world to peace.

Through Jesus Christ our Lord.

III

O Thou who hast endowed faith with power to overcome the
world, increase our faith. Help us at the beginning of this holiest
of weeks to examine again our commitments, assumptions and
loyalties. Let the figure of Jesus Christ stand over us in mercy and
in judgment, measuring our sin and pointing us to grace.

Illumine the way of all who are confused.
Quiet the troubled heart.
Deliver those who are captive to mean and unworthy purposes.
Companion the bereaved,
and comfort the dying.

Expand our horizons, O God, lest the trials of the moment close
us in to despair, and shut us out from the certainties that belong
to all who love Thee and look for Thine appearing.

And as these mercies come, we will turn with thanks to Thee the
giver.

Through Jesus Christ our Lord. *Amen.*

Maundy Thursday

I

Help us, gracious Father, with open minds and contrite hearts to
feel our way into the meaning and mystery of this night: *day*
> Quicken our imagination to the end that what went on in that
> Upper Room may come alive for us.
> For we would sit at table with the Twelve and open ourselves to
> the close-up presence of the Christ.

"The Lord Jesus, the same night in which He was betrayed, took
bread."
> We marvel at the mastery of one who on the evening of His
> own demise could avoid all thoughts of self and bend to the
> task of breaking bread for others.
> So strong in us is the urge to "get even" that we can scarcely
> fathom sharing food and drink with one whom we know in-
> tends to do us harm.
> So brittle is our faith in the providence of God that we can only
> stand and stare when one whose ways are perfect shuns all
> complaining in His final hours and meekly asks Thy blessing
> on the meal.

God, we do not sit in judgment on the Twelve for having hassled
with each other over which was greatest, for pride has often
marred our work for Thee.

We are not surprised that one by one that night they asked, when
betrayal was announced, "Is it I?":
> for, like us, they knew full well that under ample provocation
> any one of them could cash their Master in!

Let this *day* night be for us a *day* night of resolution.
Bless us with a renewed and enlarged awareness of our need for
grace:
> a more honest reading of our frailty and sin;
> a hope-building confidence in the durability of bread and cup;

a stretching of soul as we contemplate a "foolishness" with Thee
that is wiser than men, and a "weakness" with Thee that is
stronger than men.

These prayers we offer in trust and thankfulness,
through Jesus Christ our Lord. *Amen.*

Good Friday

O Thou who art afflicted in the afflictions of Thy people,
We bow before Thee in these holiest of hours, awed by the mystery
of Thy suffering love.

That we should call this day Good Friday is a bafflement of language we can scarcely comprehend.
And yet, the highest good we know is strangely centered on that
lowly hill to which our souls repair when other signs give out.

Blessed be Thy name.

Forgive us that with the cross as starting point we have made of
Christian faith a bland and easygoing way of life.
Forgive us that our preference runs to Bethlehem and Joseph's
Garden, to poinsettias and lilies,
and away from Golgotha, with its rusted nails and twisted thorns.
Forgive us that we are more willing to be instructed or reformed
than we are to be redeemed.

Open us, each one, to ever new and deeper meanings in our Saviour's passion.
Grant that we may never be causual before that event which has
taxed the skills of our finest poets and musicians,
rendered preachers mute,
and gained the grudging admiration and respect of those with
little time for Thee.
Keep us, rather, reachable and pliable,
responsive to grace,
willing captives of the wonder of it all.

Stir us now to such new intentions as will enable us to die to self
and live to Christ.
For, constrained by a love at once amazing and divine, we would
embrace a weary and despairing world, and lift that world to
Thee.

Through Jesus Christ our Lord. *Amen.*

Easter Sunday

I

On this Easter season   *your*

For this day of days, O God, we bless Thy name.
With angels and archangels and all the company of heaven, we
rejoice
    that death is finished,
    that love prevails,
    that Christ is here.
Let no hesitancy in believing,
no heaviness of circumstance,
no dullness of heart,
no familiarity with Easters past,
    deprive our souls of this day's joy and peace.
            Season's

For the knowledge that neither death nor life, things present or to
come, or anything else within the whole creation can separate us
from Thy love, we laud and magnify Thy name.
   your   *praise*   *your*

Through Jesus Christ our Lord.

II

Eternal God, in whose sight all men are precious, hear us as we
pray for those whose present lot in life makes doubt easier than
faith:
    the prisoner in his cell away from those he loves;
    the addict, whose whole world turns on his next fix;
    the unemployed and underpaid, for whom survival is the only
        item on the docket;
    the morally defunct, despisers of themselves, unable to believe
        that anyone could care;
    the recently bereaved, consumed by a terrifying sense of loss;
    the highly successful, who have clawed and finessed their way
        to the top, only to find that they were happier when they
        owned less and trusted more;
    the apostate, once captured by the gospel and loyal to the Christ,
        now hostile or indifferent, yet not quite able to forget.

O Thou who art able to do for us more than ever we could ask or think; let Thy word of hope and resurrection bid once again for the hearts of all men everywhere until, in the light that streams from Joseph's Garden, we see our world, our neighbor and ourselves;

through Jesus Christ our Lord.

III

We pray, as a company of those who love Thee, that we may be given whatever it takes to run with patience the race that is set before us.
Make us the kind of Christians that invite rather than hinder faith:
disciplined and informed;
generous and compassionate;
venturesome and joyful.

After the manner of our Saviour, keep us at the side of those who need us. Thicken the ties that unite us with all who love Thee, by whatever name or sign.

Use us where and as Thou wilt,
until the fever of life is over,
and our work is done,
and we rest in Thee.

All which we pray in faith and with thanksgiving,
through Jesus Christ our Lord.   *Amen.*

Pentecost

I

Our kind and gracious heavenly father, the hope of all who seek thee, and the joy of all who find, diverse though we are in age and outlook, we are one in our desire to voice our gratitude to Thee.

We thank Thee for our time and place in history:
> for the vision of a better world, that even the baleful face of war cannot obscure;
> for the way in which our hearts keep finding in the Christ the master clue to what it's all about.

We thank Thee for dormant passages of Scripture that spring to life for us in crisis hours;
> for friends who mediate Thy caring love;
> for the staccato thrust of new truth that raps on the door of our minds and will not take "no" for an answer.

All Thy works praise Thee in all places of Thy dominion, and in that chorus we would gladly join;
> through Jesus Christ our Lord.

I I

We pray on this Day of Pentecost for the church wherever it is found. Open Thy people anew to the empowering winds of Thy Spirit, lest we look for sustenance to sources that were never meant to be our life.

Increase our confidence in the gospel as the word that makes men whole:
> our belief in the power of love to conquer hate;
> our patience to accept and work through conflict as a way of reaching peace;
> our ability to be *in* the world but not *of* it.

Teach us to sing again, who can only cry.

Teach us to dance again, who are too much given to decency and order;

Teach us to leap and run again, who have lost the first fine careless rapture of our earliest years in Christ.

Let Thy church, like a city set upon a hill, be a beacon of hope and a sign of life for an age that seems to kill the things it loves.

Bless Thy church, O God,
    with leaders who both think and feel;
    with shepherds who love their sheep;
    with theologians who balance faith and reason;
    with members whose loyalty to Christ is a seven day a week affair for life.

Grant these mercies, we beseech Thee,
    through Jesus Christ our Lord.

III

We pray, lastly, for ourselves:
    a people who live in many different worlds;
    a people capable of mischief and mercy;
    a people who on clear days have seen forever, and in dark circumstances have struggled to see at all.

O Lord, cast us not away. For all of our false starts and broken promises, we love Thee more than all.

Let the sick know that Thou art God.

Be present through the watches of the night with those who mourn.

Stay the impulsiveness of any who are toying with a self-destructive act.

Revive us, O God, in the midst of the years, and let something of Thy beauty be upon us. For we would live even as we pray, to Thy praise alone.

Through Jesus Christ our Lord. *Amen.*

Reformation Sunday

I

Our God and God of our fathers, whose love pales every other wonder of the world, we thank Thee for the ability to remember, and the influence of ages past on ages yet to come.

Most especially on this Reformation Sunday would we speak our gratitude to Thee for the faith in which we stand:
    those who have defended and amended it across the years;
    those who have guarded it against absorption into any number
      of alien cultures;
    those who have put their lives on the line in the interest of its
      truth and purity;
    those in our own generation who understand that nothing stays
      won, and work at continuing reform.
Heirs of such riches, we would bequeath as much and more to those who follow after, relying on Thy grace alone.

Through Jesus Christ our Lord.

II

We concentrate our prayers on the youth of the world who hold in common the prospect of a puzzling and uncertain future. As names and faces rush to mind we pray for our sons and daughters, and their counterparts in every land, that they may:
    continue to question old ways and systems;
    continue to work and hope for the abolition of ancient and
      stubborn wrongs;
    continue to puncture sham and pretense wherever they find it,
      even in their own hearts;
    continue to challenge the forms of faith to correspond more fully
      to their essence.

Claim for Thyself, O God, the best and brightest of our young,
endowing them with confidence in the Scriptures, and with
   the ability to dream and envision;
   the power to withstand the false gods of status and success;
   and a love for Jesus Christ that will shape their every thought
      and action and validate their witness.

All which we humbly ask,
   through Jesus Christ our Lord.

III

To look at us, dear Lord, it would appear
   that our grip on life is firm;
   that we are managing well;
   that we have come to terms with the fears and frustrations that
      have haunted men and women ever since the story started.
Yet in our own eyes, as in Thy sight, we are not the masters of our
fate that we pretend to be. We are anxious about—
   the well-being of aging loved ones;
   our children;
   our jobs;
   our health;
   our shrinking life expectancy;
   the number and power of our sins.
In a candor qualified by mercy, show us again the connection between our anxious minds and our lack of faith. So enlarge our
trust that, fearing nothing save the loss of Thee, we may take what
comes as those who have seen the end and know that it is good,
and master the secret of the carefree life, to the praise of Thy
strong name.

Through Jesus Christ our Lord.   *Amen.*